UNVARNISHED
TRUTH

UNVARNISHED TRUTH

Life's Greatest Story

BLAKE GIDEON

MASTER DESIGN PUBLISHING
Fulton, KY

          Master Design Publishing
          789 State Route 94 E
          Fulton, KY 42041
          www.masterdesign.org

Unless otherwise noted, all Scripture quotations are taken from the HOLMAN CHRISTIAN STANDARD BIBLE (HCSB): Scripture taken from the HOLMAN CHRISTIAN STANDARD BIBLE, copyright© 1999, 2000, 2002, 2003 by Holman Bible Publishers, Nashville Tennessee. All rights reserved.

Scriptures marked RSV are taken from the REVISED STANDARD VERSION, Grand Rapids: Zondervan, 1971.

Scriptures marked KJV are taken from the KING JAMES VERSION (KJV): KING JAMES VERSION, public domain.

This work is adapted from Bible Studies for Life, LifeWay Christian Resources. Used with permission.

Layout and Cover Design by Faithe Thomas

Printed in the USA

DEDICATION

I dedicate this book to Dr. Anthony Jordan and Bob Mayfield of Baptist General Convention of Oklahoma; without them the contents of this book would have never come to fruition. I would also like to thank LifeWay Christian Resources for their direction and initial edits.

CONTENTS

INTRODUCTION

Peel away the lies. Find the truth.

WHAT IS TRUTH?
If a man took a key and scratched down the side of your car with it, he could say: "I believe it was perfectly okay to do that. It wasn't wrong, and that's the truth." But I'm sure you would disagree with him on the definition of that truth! Such a scenario may sound absurd, yet the same approach is used constantly in our society regarding the issues of life, morality, ethics, relationships – and even death.

So we need to ask again: "What is truth?"

Winston Churchill once stated, "Men occasionally stumble over the truth, but most of them pick themselves up and hurry off as if nothing had happened."

Can anyone really know "the truth"? Or is truth subject to human interpretation?

Many today think truth is relative to the circumstances—that what is true for one situation is not necessarily true for others. This means that truth for one person is not necessarily the same for everyone! If this is correct, how can we know with certainty what to believe and how we should live?

Former President Ronald Reagan stated, "Americans yearn to explore life's deepest truths." He went on to say, "Within the covers of that single book [the Bible] are all the answers to all the problems that face us today, if we would only read and believe."

Reagan is heralded as one of America's greatest leaders. He also believed that there is a divine plan for all of us. Other world leaders have said that they held the same belief.

The night before His crucifixion, Jesus offered a heartfelt prayer to His Father on behalf of His disciples—not only those of that day, but also those who would follow Him in the future. Within the context of that prayer, He said, "Sanctify [set apart] them by Your truth. Your word is truth" (John 17:17, emphasis added throughout).

Here, Christ is saying one should be able to examine the pages of God's Word—the Holy Bible—to learn the truth on any subject of major importance or significance. The Bible contains the answers to questions about why we were born, our purpose in life, whether God exists and the potential of mankind—to name only a few of the subjects covered within that Book.

The Psalmist wrote similarly: "The entirety of Your word is truth" (Psalm 119:160). Interestingly, the word "truth" can be found more than 200 times in Scripture.

In much the same way that a person strips away layers of old paint to get to the original beauty of a priceless antique, this book seeks to remove all the layers and opinions that have clogged our culture in recent decades. My goal is to get to the unvarnished truth of what really matters. And in the process, we'll see that the truth in Christ becomes our greatest story – the one we must believe to enter a relationship with God, and the one each of us must go and tell to help others do the same.

Now more than ever, our culture needs to see the unvarnished truth about Jesus Christ. Now is the time to share the hope that truth has brought to the world.

CHAPTER ONE
ONE GREAT CREATOR

The Point:
God created us and He knows each of us.

Does God Exist?

O NE QUESTION HAS BEEN UNIVERSAL to every culture and civilization in human history: *How did we get here?*

People often attempt to answer this question by looking through two different lenses: science and religion. Unfortunately, many people have come to the conclusion that these lenses are in opposition to each other – that we must embrace one and reject the other.

The truth is that science and faith are not enemies. In fact, they should be viewed as partners. That's why I'm glad to know 72 percent of Americans – including 46 percent of non-religious Americans – believe the universe points to some form of intelligent Creator.[1] Many scientists feel the same, including brilliant minds such as Francis Collins, who was head of the National Human Genome Research Institute for 15 years. Thus, the vast majority of Americans believe that because anything exists there must be a God who brought it into existence. In other words, without a God to create it, nothing could or would exist. It is possible for God to exist without the universe, but it is not possible for the universe to exist without God.[2]

Doug Powell provides a great illustration on the reality of divine design when he writes:

> Imagine you are walking through the woods and find a watch lying on the ground. What would your first thought be? That random factors over time just happened to form a watch and then cough it up from the ground? That stray bits of metal chanced to assemble themselves in a way that just happened to be useful? That a spring was formed with no purpose and inadvertently came across a cog that was formed with no purpose and then were joined accidentally to a number of other gears, springs, and cogs, eventually forming a fully functioning and accurate instrument that could measure time? Of course not. You would assume someone had dropped

it. This is because of its obvious design features. The precision and intentionality of the mechanism betray a purpose, a plan. There must have been an intelligence who conceived of the watch and its workings and then created the watch.[3]

When we observe nature, whether on a tiny level (like cells or proteins) or on a grand scale (like whole organisms or even the universe), we can see precision and intentionality, a purpose, a plan. Thus, from that observation we can conclude that there must be an intelligence behind it all. Just like my kids when they touch my truck windows leaving their fingerprints all over it, so the fingerprint of God is all over creation.[4]

Still, acknowledging a generic "designer" won't help us on a spiritual level. We need to go deeper. Thankfully, we can learn more about our Creator by exploring the Bible, which is His Word.

God Is Real

Psalm 33:6-9

[6] *The heavens were made by the word of the Lord, and all the stars, by the breath of His mouth.* [7] *He gathers the waters of the sea into a heap; He puts the depths into storehouses.* [8] *Let the whole earth tremble before the Lord; let all the inhabitants of the world stand in awe of Him.* [9] *For He spoke, and it came into being; He commanded, and it came into existence.*

As a whole, Psalm 33 is an expression of praise to God as our Creator. When we look at verses 6-9, specifically, we see an emphasis on God's power as Creator. The heavens and all they contain were made by the spoken "word of the Lord." Indeed, God is so powerful that He created the universe out of nothing (see Heb. 11:3). His mere command resulted in the vastness and majesty of everything we see. And when we observe the beauty of God's creation, we naturally marvel at His handiwork.

God also created you. God formed you in your mother's womb so that you are fearfully and wonderfully made (Ps. 139:13-14). God created you for a purpose and you can only realize and fulfill that purpose as you follow Him. Creation itself should cause you to bow daily in submission to its Creator.

Obviously, some people challenge the reality of God's existence. Atheists deny God's existence, while agnostic are unsure. So, can we be certain that God exists? Absolutely!

The complexities of the human body offer a great deal of evidence for the existence of God. The intricacies of our biology point to divine design. And divine design, in turn, points to a divine Creator. Take DNA for an example. DNA is simply an agent used to convey and store information that is necessary for the body to develop and function. But before DNA could be useful, there had to be a language established. The genetic code had to exist prior to the existence of DNA and come from outside the DNA. Information did not emerge from DNA itself and more than a bowl of alphabet soup can spell "I LOVE YOU." The best explanation for the information found in DNA is that it was imposed on the DNA by a mind, divine intelligence, God.[5] Paul wrote, "For His invisible attributes, that is, His eternal power and divine nature, have been clearly seen since the creation of the world, being understood through what He has made" (Rom. 1:20).

Objective morality is another type of evidence for God. In general, we find that certain acts – such as murdering an innocent person – are deemed immoral in all places and in all times throughout history. Therefore, any person (including an atheist) who agrees that murder is evil has adopted an objective morality. For example, answer this question, "Was Adolph Hitler wrong for what he did to the Jews during the Holocaust?" If you say, yes, he was wrong, then you are affirming objective moralities. This brings us to my next question, where/who does absolute morality come from? This person must have power to impose all humanity with an ability to know their moral will through intuition. Thus, morality can only come from a transcendent person who has the power and authority to impose a moral law on all of us. His name is God.

In other words, the universe around us and our own conscience within us both scream, "There is a God."

Let's not miss the incredible fact that God's creation includes us! Motivated by His infinite love, God created us with moral freedom – with the ability to choose between right and wrong. Why? Because true love doesn't force itself upon someone. Freedom is a divine gift bestowed on us by our loving God. Sadly, we responded to this act of love by rebelling against our Creator, which is the essence of sin.

God Is Good

Psalm 33:13-15

13 The Lord looks down from heaven; He observes everyone. 14 He gazes on all the inhabitants of the earth from His dwelling place. 15 He alone shapes their hearts; He considers all their works.

While verses 6-9 identify God as the all-powerful Creator; verses 13-15 remind us that God is also omniscient, which means He is all-knowing. As God looks down from His throne in heaven, He sees all and knows all. Nothing escapes His notice.

That thought might strike fear in us, but it shouldn't. Why? Because God cares deeply about us. He desires for each one of us to know Him intimately. For this reason, God uses the circumstances of our lives to shape our hearts. You may not understand why you are going through what you're going through at times, but you can trust God. He is loving and infinitely good. When you place your trust in Him, you have the assurance of His divine presence and care – forever.

Think about it, how big is the universe? If you ask an astronomer, he or she will tell you that the universe contains trillions of stars, and that the most distant galaxies are billions of light-years away. Not just thousands or millions or even billions of stars, but trillions of them spread out across the vast expanse of space!

To think that the Creator who made and upholds all this immensity has focused His redemptive love on tiny creatures like us—and sinful creatures at that! He cherishes us individually as if each one were the sole object of His fatherly attention.

However, some people question God's power in light of the evil in the world. Others question His love for the same reasons. *If God is so good, then why does He allow people to suffer?* This question has a relatively simple answer: we live in a fallen world because we are stained by sin. Sin is something we choose to do. God does not choose for us to sin.

Still, even in the midst of a sinful world, God in His goodness can – and often does – use suffering in a redemptive way.

→ Joseph suffered again and again, but in the end, he told his brothers: "You planned evil against me; God planned it for good to bring about the present result – the survival of many people" (Gen. 50:20).

→ When Jesus' disciples encountered a man born blind, they asked Jesus whether it was the man's own sin or that of his parents that had caused his blindness. "Neither this man nor his parents sinned," Jesus answered. "This came about so that God's works might be displayed in him" (John 9:3).

→ The greatest example of suffering was the crucifixion of Jesus. Yet through His suffering, God brought life and salvation (see 1 Pet. 3:18).

God Is Personal

Colossians 1:15-17

15 He is the image of the invisible God, the firstborn over all creation. 16 For everything was created by Him, in heaven and on earth, the visible and the invisible, whether thrones or dominions or rulers or authorities—all things have been created through Him and for Him. 17 He is before all things, and by Him all things hold together.

We find another poem about God in Colossians 1:15-17, although this poem is centered on Jesus, who is God the Son. Let's make sure we understand that distinction before we go any further. Jesus is the Son of God, but being God's Son is more than a relational tie. Jesus is God.

God has existed throughout all of eternity as three Persons—Father, Son, and Holy Spirit. However, God chose to take on human flesh through the miraculous birth of the Son, Jesus. This is known as the "Incarnation," God coming in human flesh.

Jesus Christ is the physical manifestation of the eternal God. Jesus is the exact representation of

God because He is God (see Heb. 1:3). The term "firstborn" in verse 15 means Christ is preeminent (or most important), not that He was a created being. He is the Creator who entered creation. He is "over all creation" and "before all things." He is supreme.

Since Jesus is God, we need only look to Him to understand the character of our Creator.

→ God is powerful, as we see in the miracles of Jesus.

→ God is caring and compassionate, as we see when Jesus healed the sick, gave sight to the blind, and fed the multitudes.

→ God is holy and hates sin, as we see in Jesus' righteous anger over the desecration of God's temple (see Matt. 21:12-13).

→ God is loving and just, as we see in Jesus' death. Justice demands payment for sin. In His love, Jesus took our sin upon Himself (see 2 Cor. 5:21).

A Song To Christ

Psalm 33 and Colossians 1 are both poems that describe our Creator. Read Philippians 2:5-11, often referred to as the "Song to Christ," and record any insights these verses teach you about the nature and character of Jesus, our Creator.

⁵ Make your own attitude that of Christ Jesus,

⁶ who, existing in the form of God, did not consider equality with God as something to be used for His own advantage.

⁷ Instead He emptied Himself by assuming the form of a slave, taking on the likeness of men.

And when He had come as a man in His external form,

⁸ He humbled Himself by becoming obedient to the point of death—even to death on a cross.

⁹ For this reason God highly exalted Him and gave Him the name that is above every name,

¹⁰ so that at the name of Jesus every knee will bow—of those who are in heaven and on earth and under the earth—

¹¹ and every tongue should confess that Jesus Christ is Lord, to the glory of God the Father.

Make It Count

Your Creator is real, and He really knows everything about you. How will these truths influence your life this week? Consider taking one of the following steps as a response:

→ Evaluate. Does your life say you know God personally, or just that you know about Him? Ask some of your friends and family members to answer this question about you.

→ Study. Broaden your understanding of the scientific view of creation by reading a book such as the *Holman QuickSource Guide to Understanding Creation* (B&H, 2008).

→ Invest. All people are created by God, which means that all people have value. Be intentional about spending time with someone this week in order to bless that person and reflect God's care for His creation.

We live in a world that is increasingly reliant on science and the scientific methods. Don't let that scare you. The more science reveals to us about creation, the more we will learn about our wondrous Creator who loves us.

CHAPTER TWO

ONE GREAT PURPOSE

The Point:
We were created to glorify God and enjoy Him forever.

What is the meaning of life?

COUNTLESS PEOPLE HAVE DISCUSSED THAT question through the ages. And they've all come up with different answers. Take, for example, the conclusion of one celebrity who endured cancer and 17 months of chemotherapy and radiation. She said: "What I learned is very simple: that your life belongs to you. And it really doesn't matter what you do with it. Not what your mother or father or friends or society want. It should be 'I-directed.' And that's the only purpose for being here."[6]

Sadly, I also lived for a long time with a worldly misunderstanding of purpose. I was a very selfish person. My life was "I-directed," and I sought fulfillment in materialism, relationships, and money. These resulted in momentary satisfaction, but the emptiness always returned. I was living my life without real purpose.

Thankfully, I discovered the purpose of my life – of *our* lives – in time. That purpose is made clear in the pages of Scripture.

How Does The Bible Answer This?

Isaiah 43:1-2

> [1] *Now this is what the Lord says—the One who created you, Jacob, and the One who formed you, Israel—"Do not fear, for I have redeemed you; I have called you by your name; you are Mine.* [2] *I will be with you when you pass through the waters."*

Isaiah 43 addresses God's relationship with Israel, and it still holds great meaning for us today. Consider what verses 1-2 tell us about God's connection with His chosen people:

→ God created and formed them.

→ God redeemed them out of bondage in Egypt.

→ God called them by name; they were His possession.

Don't miss the intimacy and purpose in God's choice of words: "created," "formed," "redeemed," and "called." God created you, as well – and He created you to live in relationship with Him. If you have a relationship with the Lord, He is forming you each day to become more like Him, much as a potter forms clay (see Isa. 64:8). If you're a Christian, God has redeemed you through Jesus Christ. He has set you free from the penalty and the power of sin. He has called you by name and brought you to Himself.

He desires for you to grow beyond mere knowledge *about* Him. He wants you to know Him more and more so that you will grow deeper in your walk and relationship *with* Him. The apostle Paul reflected on this type of growth when speaking about his life goals: "My goal is to know Him and the power of His resurrection and the fellowship of His sufferings, being conformed to His death, assuming that I will somehow reach the resurrection from among the dead" (Phil. 3:10-11).

Of course there is a significant difference between those who just know about God and those who truly know Him. Let me borrow the words of J.I. Packer, "A little knowledge of God is worth more than a great deal of knowledge about Him." To focus this point further, let me say two things borrowed from Packer: (1) One can know a great deal about God without much knowledge of Him. For example, many read books and study theology and even have degrees on the subject. However, interest in theology and knowledge about God is not at all the same as knowing Him. (2)

One can know a great deal about godliness without much knowledge of God. Bookstores and libraries are full of "how to" books. You can find books on how to tithe your money, how to be a young Christian, how to lead people to Christ, how to pray, as you can see the list could go on.[7]

On the other hand, those who truly know God, have great energy for God. Packer provides the following insight. In one of the prophetic chapters of Daniel we read, "...the people that do know their God shall be strong and do exploits" (11:32 KJV). The RSV renders thus: "the people who know their God shall stand firm and take action." This shows the action taken by those who know God in the face of anti-God trends. While their God is being defied or disregarded, they cannot rest; they feel they must do something. The dishonor done to God's name goads them to action. Furthermore, those who know God have great thoughts of God. Their thoughts are as those of Daniel who prayed, "Praise be to the name of God for ever and ever; wisdom and power are His. He changes times and seasons; He sets up kings and deposes them. He gives wisdom. He knows what lies in darkness and light dwells with Him" (Daniel 2:20-22).

It should also go without saying that those who truly know God, demonstrate great boldness for God. Daniel and his friends were men who stuck their necks out. This was not foolhardiness. They knew what they were doing. They had counted the cost. They had measured the risk. They were well aware what the outcome of their actions would be unless God miraculously intervened. But they were unmoved and were willing to die for God. Lastly, those who know God have great contentment in God. There is no peace like the peace of those whose minds are possessed with full assurance that they have known God, and God has known them, and that this relationship guarantees God's favor to them in life, through death and on forever.[8]

Therefore, those in a true relationship with God can have confidence in the great promises He has given us. For example, He promises to always be with us and protect us if we know Him.

In Isaiah 43, the prophet used word pictures to describe the adversity we face in life: water and rivers, fire and flame. Yet, even in difficult trials and circumstances, God has promised to be with His people. It's encouraging to know the God who redeemed us in the past will protect us from harm in the future, no matter how difficult our situations may be.

Can you remember a time in your life when God used specific trials to teach you more about Himself?

Isaiah 43:3-4

[3] For I Yahweh your God, the Holy One of Israel, and your Savior, give Egypt as a ransom for you, Cush and Seba in your place. [4] Because you are precious in My sight and honored, and I love you,

I will give people in exchange for you and nations instead of your life.

God's promises are motivated by His love. His people are so precious in His sight that He would save them at a high price. God promised to bring them back from exile and restore them to their land. Others would experience defeat – Egypt, Cush, and Seba in this case – but the Lord would restore His people.

Not only did God promise His protection and His presence for the Israelites, but also His prosperity. In fact, God has promised prosperity to all who follow Him – but not a materialistic prosperity. We prosper with spiritual blessings: "Praise the God and Father of our Lord Jesus Christ, who has blessed us in Christ with every spiritual blessing in the heaven" (Eph. 1:3).

The greatest expression of God's love was displayed at the cross. Jesus willingly went to the cross and died as a substitute for our sins. We did nothing to earn or deserve this act of love. God has extended it to us by grace. Thankfully, just as we can do nothing to earn this loving gift from God, we can do nothing to lose it (see Rom. 8:35-39). Our salvation is eternally secure in Christ.

One of the most difficult times in my life was when I lost my dad to cancer. It was gut-wrenching, but God was with me through it all. In fact, I am closer to God as a result of what I experienced in that terrible time. What could have overtaken me, God used to draw me closer to Himself. His love was with me constantly.

That's an important principle. To enjoy the love of God doesn't mean we face every life situation with a smile on our faces, but it does mean we face every life situation with the assurance of God's presence, protection, and everlasting love. That is true prosperity.

What steps can you take to recognize and more fully enjoy God's love?

Isaiah 43:5-7

[5] Do not fear, for I am with you; I will bring your descendants from the east, and gather you from the west. [6] I will say to the north: Give them up! and to the south: Do not hold them back! Bring My sons from far away, and My daughters from the ends of the earth— [7] everyone called by My name and created for My glory. I have formed him; indeed, I have made him.

Because we were created to know and enjoy God's love, we ultimately have nothing to fear. Isaiah prophesied to the nation of Israel that, even though they would face difficulty of exile, God would bring them back home. He would be with them and His presence would keep them during their trial.

God's loving protection applies to "everyone called by My name and created for My glory." That includes us. To be created for God's glory means we are to display His character.

Isaiah 43 highlights three important attributes of God:

→ **God is love (v. 4).** We express God's love by putting others before ourselves.

Perhaps the greatest expressing of God's love is when we choose to forgive someone we feel is underserving. After all, that's what God did for us.

→ **God is holy (v. 3).** As Christians, we pursue holiness by living in obedience to God's Word.

→ **God is gracious (v. 7).** He called us by name and us for His glory – and we did nothing to deserve this. We can exemplify God's grace by extending grace to others.

When we faithfully display the character of God, our lives point to Him and bring Him glory. The gospel provides us with all the motivation and power we need to pursue this purpose wholeheartedly. God created you, called, and redeemed you. Through Christ's work on the cross, He did for us what we could not do ourselves. He brought us back to the place of living for His glory and enjoying Him forever.

What a great purpose for life! But we only experience this purpose when we submit our lives to Christ for salvation. God told His people, "Do not fear, for I am with you." And that's the key: God's presence. Sin keeps us from knowing God personally, but God demonstrated His love for us by sending His Son to die in our place (see Rom. 5:6-8).

I used to be "I-directed," but God pursued me. He called me by name. He redeemed me. He changed my life. He helped me find what I was created for – and He can do the same for you.

What does it look like to know and glorify God in our everyday lives?

What you are is God's gift to you.
What you can become is your gift to Him.
Henrietta C. Mears

Make It Count

You have a purpose. How will that truth influence your actions and attitudes this week? Consider the following options:

→ Reflect on the grace of God in your own life this week. Write down specific things God has done for you. Spend time in prayer thanking Him.

→ Display the character of God in your life this week. Look for opportunities to display the character of Jesus toward others. Perhaps you need to offer someone forgiveness. Or you can offer an act of kindness to a stranger in need.

→ Talk with someone this week about a specific way God has shown His grace to you. Be prepared to share the gospel with them if the conversation moves in that direction.

The true meaning of your life – the true purpose – is to know God and glorify Him through your life. That's a difficult decision to make, and you must make it each day. Thankfully, it's a decision that allows you to enjoy God's presence for all time.

CHAPTER THREE
ONE GREAT PROBLEM

The Point:
Without Christ, we are condemned forever.

SOME THINGS FAIL TO LIVE up to their intended purpose.

When the city of Vancouver, British Columbia purchased its first motorized ambulance in 1909, it paid a huge sum of $4,000. (That's close to $100,000 by today's standards.) Yet when the city took the ambulance on a test run, they hit a pedestrian – and killed him. This expensive purchase, meant to save lives, ended up transporting its first passenger to the morgue.

God created us for a specific purpose: to live in a joyous relationship with Him and bring Him glory. Like the ambulance, however, we have not lived up to that purpose. The Bible teaches us clearly where the problem lies – inside our hearts.

Thankfully, the Bible is also clear on the only answer to our great problem. We can read about that answer in Romans 3.

How Does The Bible Answer This?

Romans 3:9-12

> [9] What then? Are we any better? Not at all! For we have previously charged that both Jews and Gentiles are all under sin, [10] as it is written: "There is no one righteous, not even one. [11] There is no one who understands; there is no one who seeks God. [12] All have turned away; all alike have become useless. There is no one who does what is good, not even one."

In the opening chapters of the Book of Romans, Paul identified those who have sinned and are under the wrath of God. He included the kinds of people we'd expect – blatant sinners and rebellious people. But he also included people whom most of his readers would have considered to be good and religious; that is, the Jews. For centuries, the Jewish people had enjoyed special privileges as a result of being God's chosen people. Despite these privileges, however, they were still guilty of sin. (Paul was a Jew himself, which is why he asked, "Are we any better?") Both

Jews and Gentiles are guilty before God. All people everywhere are under the curse of sin and our world is in its conditions of our sin.

Evil runs rampant among us because humanity, as a whole, loves sin and despises righteousness. Many want to blame God, but the blame is ours. We all have turned away from God in order to seek sinful pleasure for ourselves. Paul referred to the Old Testament when he wrote, "There is no one righteous, not even one" (see also Ps. 14:1-3; 53:1-3; Eccl. 7:20).

No one does good? No one. Even our human attempts at goodness – trying to be good apart from God – fall woefully short. Everything we seek to do is tainted by sin. The evidence is overwhelming. It's all around us. Every day we lie, lust, disobey, covet, steal, and the list goes on. We look at the gross and obvious sins of society around us, and we tend to define sin in terms of those actions. We fail to see that our anxiety, our discontentment, our negativity, our ingratitude toward God, our pride and selfishness, our critical and judgmental attitudes toward others, our gossip, our unkind words to or about others, our preoccupation with the things of this life, and a whole host of subtle sins are an expression of rebellion against God and a despising of His Word and Person.

Sadly, much of humanity is spiritually ignorant about its sinfulness against God. Because our nature drifts so easily toward sin, we easily turn our backs on God. As a result, we have no desire either to know God or to seek Him.

Think about this: no one had to teach you how to sin. We're all born with a sinful nature. We inherited this nature from our first father, Adam, the head of the human race (see Rom. 5:12). When he fell into sin, we fell, too. Once the corruption of sin became part of humanity, the sinful nature has since passed down from generation to generation. Now, everyone is born with a sinful nature and are objects of God's wrath.

In short, we've all broken the commandments of God. We've all fallen short of Christ's righteous standard. Sin reigns in our hearts.

Romans 3:19-20

> [19] *Now we know that whatever the law says speaks to those who are subject to the law, so that every mouth may be shut and the whole world may become subject to God's judgment.* [20] *For no one will be justified in His sight by the works of the law, because the knowledge of sin comes through the law.*

Many of the Jews in Paul's day would have quickly affirmed that sinfulness was a major problem – for the Gentiles. But they never would have claimed the same problem for themselves. They were God's chosen people. They had been given God's Law.

Similarly, our world is filled with people who compare themselves with others to elevate their own righteousness: "It's not like I've ever killed anyone," or "I'm not nearly as bad as that person."

We're quick to compare ourselves with those we consider worse than we are. However, when we compare ourselves with Christ – the only true standard of righteousness – we always fall miserably short.

Jesus shines a harsh light on the reality of our own sinfulness. That's because only Jesus perfectly obeyed the law of God.

> Prostitutes are in no danger of finding their present life so satisfactory that they cannot turn to God. The proud, the avaricious, the self-righteous are in that danger.
>
> C. S. Lewis

When we say, "I am not perfect," we are admitting that we fall short of Jesus' moral standards. We are guilty of sin.

The evidence stacked against us regarding sin is overwhelming – and we have no defense. So-called "moral" people might argue, "But I do good things." Religious people might add, "I go to church." Yet no matter how moral or religious we may be, we all stand guilty of sin before a Holy God.

And here's the really bad news: guilt always leads to judgment. When it comes to our sin, the evidence has been presented, and the Judge has handed down His verdict. No amount of good works can change it. Humanity stands justly condemned before a Holy God.

This is a hard truth to accept. It flies in the face of our human pride, especially prideful cry of our modern culture: "How dare someone tell me I can't do something!" "Who are you to judge me?" "That may be true for you, but not for me." Such protests don't change the reality of our situation.

As long as we think we are good enough or strong enough to overcome sin in our own power, we cannot be saved. We're lost. And as long as we look to ourselves instead of to the only solution God has provided, we remain guilty and condemned. "Anyone who believes in Him is not condemned, but anyone who does not believe is already condemned, because he has not believed in the name of the One and Only Son of God" (John 3:18).

Romans 3:23

> 23 *For all have sinned and fall short of the glory of God.*

Our sinfulness is further magnified by the reality that we "fall short of the glory of God." Our very purpose is connected to the glory of God. He created us to bring Him glory – to be motivated only by the desire to glorify Him. Yet, the very thing He created us to do, we fail to do.

When we're not satisfied in God, we look to other things to fill the void in our hearts. We look to the things of this world, and we seek this glory for ourselves. This only leads to further emptiness because self-glory can never satisfy the soul. It is only when we live for God's glory that our souls become satisfied.

When have you felt the reality of sin in your own life?

What exactly is God's glory? The glory of God is wrapped up in the totality of who He is and what He does. When we put all God's attributes together, we see His glory. His eternal nature holiness, love, righteousness, justice, grace, wisdom, mercy, omniscience, omnipotence, and omnipresence all point to His glory. His full glory is something we can't fully fathom in this life, but we do see it in Jesus Christ. "The Son is the radiance of God's glory and the exact expression of His nature" (Heb. 1:3a).

To say that we "fall short of His glory," means we fail to measure up to the righteousness of Christ. The law served as God's standard for righteousness, but only Christ fully kept that standard. We can't come up to the standard of Christ or His perfect obedience; we fall short. But when we trust in Him, His righteousness is credited to us.

Trying to match God's standard of righteousness on our own is like trying to swim the Atlantic Ocean. Some may make it further than others, but even the world's best swimmer would eventually drown. In the same way, no matter how good you try to be, you still fall short of God's righteous standard.

Thankfully, He has not left us on our own to drown. We have hope and an answer.

How does sin prevent us from living in a way that glories God?

Make It Count

Without Christ, you are condemned forever because of your sin. How will you respond to that truth in the days to come? Consider the following options:

→ **Confess.** Ask God to reveal any areas of sin in your life that have not been dealt with. Confess those sins and do whatever is necessary to turn away from them.

→ **Pray.** Pray specifically each day for God's strength.

→ **Worship.** Spend 30 minutes this week praising God for His offer of grace and forgiveness. Thank Him for the work of Christ in your life and in the lives of those you love.

The city of Vancouver spent the equivalent of $100,000 in an effort to save lives. Christ paid a much greater price to save those who had no hope of saving themselves – including you and me.

CHAPTER FOUR
ONE GREAT SAVIOR

The Point:
God offers us hope and forgiveness
through Jesus Christ.

"IT WAS A DARK AND stormy night." That sentence is considered the classic opening for a bad novel. But it's also a scenario you don't want to experience when you've been knocked off a boat in the Gulf of Mexico. Trust me.

As a young man, I worked on an offshore drilling rig. On this particular "dark and stormy night," I was offloading materials from a supply boat. The small craft was being violently tossed in the waves when a cable hit me and launched me overboard. The pounding waves carried me further into the dark waters of the Gulf. I drifted so far that I no longer could see the lights of the rig.

After two hours went by, I gave up hope of being saved. I was lost in the darkness and gripped with fear. Suddenly a light burst through the turbulent waves – a boat equipped with a searchlight. When that light hit me, my hope was restored. I was saved!

Darkness, fear, separation, and hopelessness. That's also an apt description for being spiritually lost. But as we'll see in Romans 5, we still have hope because of Christ.

How Does The Bible Answer This?

Romans 5:6-8

6 For while we were still helpless, at the appointed moment, Christ died for the ungodly. 7 For rarely will someone die for a just person—though for a good person perhaps someone might even dare to die. 8 But God proves His own love for us in that while we were still sinners, Christ died for us!

Let me get right to the point: Jesus is the Light of the world. He dispels the darkness of our lives, removes all fear, reconciles us to God, and brings us hope. Jesus did all of this through His death on the cross – and He did it for the least likely group of people imaginable.

Paul notes three kinds of people in these verses:

→ **The just person.** Paul is not using a theological term at this point but describing a person others see as morally upright or exemplary in his or her conduct.

→ **The good person.** This person is generous, kind, and loving toward others. While the just person appears to never do anything wrong, the good person is simply someone everyone likes to be around. It's conceivable that someone might possibly die for that kind of person.

→ **The sinner.** The ones Jesus died for are neither upright nor good. They are corrupted by sin. "Christ died for the ungodly" – and this title fits all of us.

The apostle Paul placed great emphasis on the love and grace of God. Heroism might motivate someone to die for a good person, but only unmerited grace and unconditional love can drive people to die for their enemies. Jesus did just that. He died for the helpless, the ungodly, the sinners, He died for us. He died for our sins. Christ died in our place as our substitute and representative. Just as God appointed Adam to act as representative of all humanity, so He appointed Jesus Christ to act on behalf of all who trust in Him. There is no better Scripture to see the idea of substitution than this one:

Surely *He* has borne *our* griefs
    and carried *our* sorrows;
yet we esteemed *Him* stricken,
    smitten of God, and afflicted.

But *He* was wounded for *our* transgressions;
>*He* was crushed for *our* iniquities;
upon *Him* was the chastisement that brought *us* peace,
>and with *His* wounds *we* are healed.
All *we* like sheep have gone astray;
>*we* have turned every one to his own way;
and the Lord has laid on *Him*
>the iniquity of *us* all. (Isa. 53:4-6)

Note the repeated contrast which the Spirit-inspired prophet draws between the words "He" and "our", or "Him" and "us". Surely any unbiased reader cannot fail to see in the passage the idea that Jesus suffered as our substitute, bearing the punishment for sin that we deserve.[9]

What do these verses teach us about God's character?

Romans 5:9

>[9] *Much more then, since we have now been declared righteous by His blood, we will be saved through Him from wrath.*

In Christ we are "declared righteous." The Greek word for this phrase is a legal term that simply means "declared not guilty." When we follow Jesus, our sin – all of it – is removed, and we stand before God completely forgiven, justified, and righteous in His eyes.

Don't miss that word "wrath." Because God is holy, He must punish sin. In fact, His righteous character demands that He deal with our sin. Justice demands payment. However, in an act of divine love, God sent Jesus to suffer and die in our place. Christ willingly came to die as the substitute for our sin. By His death and shed blood, He is able to declare us righteous. At the cross, Christ extinguished the wrath of God toward believing sinners by His own bloody death, thereby paying the full legal debt due sinners. The result, with the penalty paid, the justice of God was forever satisfied and sinners united to Christ have been justly forgiven (declared not guilty), and justified (declared righteous).

In eastern Afghanistan, children make money from recycling used shell casings they find lying on roads. As a military convoy headed down one particular road, several soldiers jumped out of their vehicles to move the children out of the way before the heavy trucks came along.

After the children were on the side of the road, one young girl ran back to pick up another shell casing. Unfortunately, she ran out in front of a 16-ton armored truck. National Guard Sgt. Dennis Weichel saw this and ran to get her out of the way. He got her to safety – but not before he was hit by the truck. The 29-year-old from Rhode Island died just weeks after arriving in Afghanistan.[10]

This is similar to what Christ did for us, only we're not innocent children. We're the enemy. Because of our sin, the wrath of God was barreling down on us. But Christ came as our Rescuer. He absorbed the full brunt of our punishment. In doing so, He gave us not only the chance to see our sins forgiven, but also the gift of hope.

To what degree do you feel at peace in your relationship with God?

Anyone can devise a plan by which good people
Go to heaven. Only God can devise a plan
whereby sinners , which are His enemies,
can go to heaven.
Lewis Sperry Chafer

Romans 5:10-11

[10] *For if, while we were enemies, we were reconciled to God through the death of His Son, then how much more, having been reconciled, will we be saved by His life!* [11] *And not only that, but we also rejoice in God through our Lord Jesus Christ. We have now received this reconciliation through Him.*

Here we find Paul making an argument from the greater to the lesser. Since Christ declared us righteous even while we were ungodly sinners, then He will certainly save us from God's wrath now that we are His righteous children. The first truth increases the likelihood and power of the second truth.

Through His death, Christ has provided the way for peace between the sinner the Creator. The dividing wall has been torn down between God and humanity.

For this reason, Paul wrote, "How much more, having been reconciled, will we be saved by His life!" We can be even more certain of the salvation He provided because He has risen from the dead and is alive forever.

Let's look deeper at the word "reconciled." To reconcile something is to reestablish a relationship. Jesus brought reconciliation in order to reestablish the peace that humanity enjoyed with God before Adam gave in to temptation and brought sin into the world. We don't have the ability to reestablish our relationship with God, but Christ is able – and He took the initiative to make it happen.

With that in mind, to be reconciled to God means:

➜ Our future is secure. We are reconciled to God by Jesus' death, but our security is in His life. Jesus rose triumphantly from the dead, and His bodily resurrection is the proof that His rescue mission was successful. Paul wrote in I Corinthians 15:3-4, "For I passed on to you as most important what I also received: that Christ died for our sins according to the Scriptures, that He was buried, that He was raised on the third day according to the Scriptures."

➜ We have a reason for joy. Look again at Romans 5:11: "We also rejoice in God through our Lord Jesus Christ." True joy is knowing our sins are forgiven and we are at peace with God. The ultimate source of this joy is the hope we have in Christ.

The same hope, joy, and secure future are available to all who repent of sin and surrender their lives to Jesus as Lord and Savior.

Sadly, countless people around the world and in our communities are lost, and they don't even realize it. They need to reach out and receive God's forgiveness for their sins. They need to take hold of the hope and purpose they've been searching for all their lives. They need Jesus.

We can actively seek out those who need to be rescued and reconciled to God. Indeed, Christians have been entrusted with the ministry of reconciliation: "That is, in Christ, God was reconciling the world to Himself, not counting their trespasses against them, and He has committed the message of reconciliation to us. Therefore, we are ambassadors for Christ, certain that God is appealing through us. We plead on Christ's behalf, 'Be reconciled to God'" (2 Cor. 5:19-20).

When soldiers come home from war, the people who love them are at the airport waiting to greet them. When you go home to be with the Lord, who'll be at the gates for you because you played a part in their eternal destiny?[11]

If you know Jesus as your Savior, then you are an ambassador for His kingdom. You have work to do. So what are you waiting for?

In what ways does your life reflect joy in God?

Make It Count

How will you respond to God's offer of hope and forgiveness for all people? Consider the following options:

→ Write your testimony. Write out the story of your own salvation. Focus on three questions: (1) What was your life like before salvation? (2) How did you come to know Jesus? (3) What is your life like now since you've been saved?

→ Share your testimony. Pray for the opportunity to share your testimony with someone who needs to hear it. Commit to sharing the truth of the gospel with at least one person before your next group gathering.

→ Invite people. Invite someone to church with you next week.

Drifting alone and frightened in the Gulf of Mexico is bad. But drifting through life in the spiritual darkness of sin is much, much worse. Seek out Jesus, the Light of the world.

CHAPTER FIVE
ONE GREAT COMMITMENT

The Point:
To be saved, I must trust in Christ.

L IFE IS FULL OF DECISIONS. Lots of them. Columbia researcher Sheena Iyengar estimates that we make about 70 decisions every day. Do the math and that's around 25,500 decisions a year – or about 1,788,500 decisions if you live 70 years.[12]

→ Some decisions come easy. *Yes, I will marry you!*

→ Some decisions carry small consequences. *Do I order the chicken salad or the tuna salad?*

→ Some decisions bring lots of stress. *Do I take the better job even though the move will uproot my family?*

The biggest decisions are life-changing, even eternal. The greatest decision we will ever make centers on what we do with Jesus Christ. Knowing about Jesus is not enough. Our need for salvation is answered in Jesus, but we each must decide whether we will commit to that truth and trust Him – or not.

In his letter to the Romans, Paul emphasized the critical importance of this decision. It's the choice of a lifetime.

How Does The Bible Answer This?

Romans 10:1-3

[1] Brothers, my heart's desire and prayer to God concerning them is for their salvation! [2] I can testify about them that they have zeal for God, but not according to knowledge. [3] Because they disregarded the righteousness from God and attempted to establish their own righteousness, they have not submitted themselves to God's righteousness.

The Jewish people of Paul's day had a great "zeal for God," so why didn't they already have salvation? Because their zeal was "not according to knowledge." The Jews believed they had good standing with God because of the law, their religious traditions, and their religious activity. They were sincere in their endeavors, but their sincerity was tragically misplaced. No matter how hard they tried, they could never be good enough to earn favor with God.

They weren't alone in their zeal without knowledge. At the core of most religions is the belief that people are basically good and can work their way to God. Even in the church, a lot of people fill their lives with religious activities and good morals, thinking these things will give them a connection to God. But merely being a religious person is not good enough.

This is what makes Christianity unique. Christianity focuses on what Jesus did. Other religions focus on what we should do. God came down to Earth in the Person of Jesus and lived a sinless life. In His perfect righteousness He took our sin on Himself, willingly went to the cross, and died in our place. Then He rose three days later from the grave, having defeated sin and death. For this reason, there is no other way of salvation: Christ alone saves.

Jesus said: "I am the way, the truth, and the life. No one comes to the Father except through Me" (John 14:6).

Christians are saved because of the blood of Christ. If that weren't amazing enough, when we trust Jesus for salvation, His righteousness is credited to our account. No one else can do this for us. No one else died to save us. Christ alone saves.

Where in our culture do we often see zeal without knowledge?

The answer we need is all wrapped up in Jesus. But knowing about Jesus is not enough. Having a zeal for God – or even knowing the truth about Jesus – does not guarantee salvation. We have to act on that knowledge.

Romans 10:8b-10

> *8 On the contrary, what does it say? The message is near you, in your mouth and in your heart This is the message of faith that we proclaim: 9 If you confess with your mouth, "Jesus is Lord," and believe in your heart that God raised Him from the dead, you will be saved. 10 One believes with the heart, resulting in righteousness, and one confesses with the mouth, resulting in salvation.*

If knowing the truth about Jesus isn't enough what do we need to do? Paul used two verbs to give us the answer.

→ **Confess with your mouth.** "Jesus is Lord." To confess something means literally "to speak the same thing." The word "Lord" comes from the Greek work kurios, which signifies Jesus' sovereign power and authority. So, when we confess, we are agreeing with God that Jesus is the sovereign Lord with authority over all – including our lives. We further agree with God by living in submission to the rule of Jesus.

→ **Believe in your heart that God raised Him from the dead.** To believe in the death of Jesus doesn't go far enough. I know Jesus is Lord because even death cannot hold Him. He died for me, but He is alive because God raised Him. Without the resurrection, Jesus would have been just a really good man who died a very tragic death. The fact that separates Jesus from all other religious leaders is that Jesus died and rose from the dead – and is alive today. God approved of Jesus' sacrifice by raising Him from the dead, and He is the one and only Lord.

What are the implications of confessing Jesus as Lord?

Confess and believe. We shouldn't view these as two separate actions. One is an inward belief and the other is an outward confession, but you really can't have one without the other. They are two sides of the same coin.

When you fully believe in your heart, you can't help but confess and live out the belief.

Confessing and believing are not a form of "easy believism." Far from it. "Easy believism" teaches grace without repentance, salvation without commitment. Many want Jesus to save them from hell, but they don't want to live their lives for Him. But we can't accept Jesus as our Savior without embracing Him as Lord.

Submitting to Christ's lordship is essential for salvation. When we confess Christ as Lord, we are essentially saying: "Jesus, You alone are sovereign. You alone have all power. You alone are my Master.

Therefore, I surrender to You. My life is no longer mine – it's Yours."

What makes salvation both easy and difficult?

Romans 10:11-13

> [11] Now the Scripture says, Everyone who believes on Him will not be put to shame, [12] for there is no distinction between Jew and Greek, since the same Lord of all is rich to all who call on Him. [13] For everyone who calls on the name of the Lord will be saved.

Who is able to confess and believe in Jesus? Anyone and everyone. The gospel is for Jew and Gentile alike, "everyone" who demonstrates the openness of God's call to salvation. God makes no distinction between people; He desires for all people to be saved. Salvation is available for all people regardless of ethnicity, race, or background.

The only requirement is that every individual must trust in Christ to receive that salvation. God's salvation is for all people by grace through faith in Christ. "The same Lord of all is rich to all who call on Him."

God is rich to all! It's not that He responds to everyone who prays a prayer, or extends special favor only to certain people, such as the Jews or those who are especially upright or religious. No. God extends His riches – all the blessings of living in His presence – to everyone who calls on His name. But how do we call on Him? We call on Him by exercising faith in the crucified and risen Son of God, Jesus Christ, as the Savior and Lord and Treasure of our lives. What salvation requires is faith.

Those who call on the name of Jesus are changed, regardless of who they are (or who they used to be). I recently worked alongside a Japanese believer to share the gospel in Brazil. During the same time, a group from my church worked alongside believers from Nepal to reach kids in Kansas City through Vacation Bible School. This is a great expression of the power and extent of the gospel. The gospel extends around the world to save Americans, Brazilians, and Nepalese. Everyone.

Any of us can come to faith in Christ – and we can share that faith with anyone. And we must share our faith. Because salvation in Christ is the only hope for a lost world. Therefore, I plead with you on behalf of Christ, believe on the Lord Jesus Christ. Receive Him as the Savior and Lord.

How has the gospel changed your life?

"The gospel is open to all.
The most respectful sinner has no more
claim on it than the worst."
Dr. Martin Lloyd Jones

Make It Count

What actions will you take this week in light of the truth that salvation comes through faith in Jesus Christ alone? Consider the following suggestions:

→ **Accept**. If you have not yet believed in Jesus and confessed Him as Lord, do so now. Trust Him for forgiveness from your sin. Turn to Him for a new life.

→ **Examine**. Make time this week to assess your relationship with Jesus. Are you studying His Word? Are you sharing the truth of the gospel with others?

→ **Start**. Help launch a new Bible study in your church, neighborhood, or community with the purpose of reaching those who need to hear the truth about Jesus.

You're going to make around 70 decisions today. Be sure to make one that has the potential to be life-changing, either for you or for someone you know.

CHAPTER SIX
ONE GREAT TASK

The Point:
Each of us must share the gospel.

" I HAVE TWO KINDS OF problems: the urgent and the important. The urgent are not important, and the important are never urgent." President Dwight D. Eisenhower spoke these words in 1954 to a gathering of church leaders.[13] It's interesting to hear those words coming from a man who had to make major decisions every day.

When you think about it, though, few things truly fall into both categories.

➙ Exercise is important, but not urgent.

➙ An email message can be extremely urgent, but not necessarily important.

Of course, some things really are both urgent and important. One example is a medical emergency. Another example is the task given to every disciple of Jesus: sharing the good news of Christ with others. People have no more important decision to make than to choose Christ, and now is the time for us to point them to Christ and help them understand everything at stake. What is God's plan for reaching others with the gospel?

How Does The Bible Answer This?

2 Timothy 2:1-2

> ¹You, therefore, my son, be strong in the grace that is in Christ Jesus. ² And what you have heard from me in the presence of many witnesses, commit to faithful men who will be able to teach others also.

What Paul described in these verses is the process of discipleship, which involves knowing and walking in the truths of Jesus and leading others to do the same. To disciple someone, then, begins with helping them to know and embrace the good news of Jesus Christ. All of this is reflected in the Great Commission Jesus gave His disciples at the end of His earthly ministry: "Go, therefore and make disciples of all nations, baptizing them in the name of the Father and of the Son and of the Holy Spirit, teaching them to obey everything I have commanded you. And remember I am with you always, to the end of the age" (Matt. 28:19-20).

Paul had invested much time and effort in teaching and discipling Timothy. Now, he encouraged Timothy to pay it forward, investing in others who would "teach others also." Paul told Timothy to invest his life in men who had proven their love for the Lord. Once these men were faithfully trained, they in turn were obligated to invest in others. This is God's method of multiplication. Each disciple is entrusted with the gospel and has a responsibility to share it with others.

Joseph Brucato is a great example of what goes wrong when we don't take discipleship seriously. Brucato was a mailman in Brooklyn, New York. One day, his supervisor happened to walk past the mailman's personal car and saw it was full of mail. The supervisor confronted him, and Brucato admitted that he sometimes didn't deliver all the mail. He blamed alcohol and depression. When postal inspectors went to his apartment, they found 40,000 pieces of undelivered mail – some 2,500 pounds![14]

Who has been faithful in teaching you the truth about God and the gospel?

The missing mail included several personal messages – many of which were both important and urgent. But because the mail was never delivered, people were robbed of what they needed to hear.

Sadly many Christians do something far more outrageous than hoarding mail; they hoard the good news of Christ.

Paul's challenge to Timothy echoes the Great Commission. In the same way Paul shared Christ with Timothy and discipled him, Timothy could share Christ and disciple others. And because someone shared Christ with us, we can do the same for others. In fact, we must do the same for others.

Some people want salvation but don't want to put in the time to be strong disciples of Jesus Christ. What many Christians want to do is audit the Christian life. An audit is where a person goes to class to get information, but is not required to do any of the work. They don't have to take a test or do any homework. They are only attending for informational purposes. They want the data without the responsibility. That's an audit. This is what some people do every Sunday. They audit Jesus.[15] We are not called to audit Jesus or Christianity. We are called and mandated to "make disciples."

2 Timothy 2:1-2

[3] Share in suffering as a good soldier of Christ Jesus. [4] No one serving as a soldier gets entangled in the concerns of civilian life; he seeks to please the recruiter. [5] Also, if anyone competes as an athlete, he is not crowned unless he competes according to the rules. [6] The hardworking farmer ought to be the first to get a share of the crops. [7] Consider what I say, for the Lord will give you understanding in everything.

Sharing the good news of Christ isn't always easy. In fact, sometimes it's downright hard – perhaps even dangerous. We are to persevere, however, even if doing so brings challenges.

Paul gave Timothy three examples of people who persevere:

→ **The soldier.** A soldier's one duty is to obey his commanding officer. And, like good soldiers, we are to persevere in our obedience to Christ. Our primary goal is to please Him, even when it requires us to go on the front lines of spiritual warfare.

→ **The athlete.** Paul likely was familiar with the Olympic games. In his day, athletes trained in the presence of the judges during the month before the games. If an athlete violated the rules, the judges imposed corporal punishment or heavy fines. To be victorious, the athlete needed diligence, self-control, and discipline.

→ **The farmer.** A hardworking farmer should get to enjoy the compensations of his produce. But he has to persevere in working his crops for months before he sees the fruit of his labor. The faithful witness also may get to enjoy the fruits of his or her labor by seeing people come to faith in Christ.

What can we learn from Paul's word pictures in these verses?

There is no joy in all the world like that of
Bringing one soul to Christ.
William Barclay

Sharing Christ isn't easy. It takes focus, discipline, and hard work – but the payoffs make it all worth it.

Let me tell you about Azzam, a Christian in Somalia who has a passion for sharing the gospel and God's Word. Unfortunately, he must smuggle Bibles into his country, and the only way he's been able to do this is in coffins. Azzam will actually climb into a coffin and lie underneath a deceased body. He travels this way to Kenya, where he gets Bibles. Then he finds another coffin headed to Somalia and travels back home with the Bibles. Azzam said: "I love the irony that caskets for dead people are used by God to bring new life in Somalia! Many are being transformed into the likeness of our Savior."[16]

Azzam is an inspiring example of what Paul was teaching: that we are to be disciplined, do whatever it takes, and endure suffering when necessary in order to advance the cause of Christ.

What excuses do we make for not sharing Christ?

2 Timothy 2:8-10

> [8] *Keep your attention on Jesus Christ as risen from the dead and descended from David. This is according to my gospel.* [9] *I suffer for it to the point of being bound like a criminal, but God's message is not bound.* [10] *This is why I endure all things for the elect: so that they also may obtain salvation, which is in Christ Jesus, with eternal glory.*

Jesus is the ultimate example of perseverance in faithful witnessing.

→ **Jesus is the greatest example of a soldier.** He was obedient even to death for us. He fought the ultimate battle for us – and won (see Phil. 2:8-9).

→ **Jesus is the greatest example of an athlete.** He endured until He was victorious over sin and death and gained the prize – our salvation (see Heb. 12:2).

→ **Jesus is the greatest example of a farmer.** He alone has the power to break apart the hardened soil in a person's life to bear spiritual fruit (see Matt. 13:1-23).

Paul also knew about persevering for the sake of sharing Christ. While he was writing his letter to Timothy, he was in chains in a Roman prison. Worse, he knew he soon would be put to death by his captors (see 2 Tim. 4:6). Amazingly, even in chains, Paul declared that "God's message is not bound." Paul knew he might die, but the gospel never would. In fact, the gospel of Jesus Christ had become Paul's very life; he called it "my gospel."

How do you want to spend your life? Will you persevere for the gospel, or will you wander away from your task when the going gets tough?

The choice is yours.

What steps can you take this month to share the gospel with the ultimate goal of making a disciple?

John Piper tells the following story: I will tell you what a tragedy is. I will show you how to waste your life. Consider a story from the February 1998 edition of *Reader's Digest*, which tells about a couple who "took early retirement from their jobs in the Northeast five years ago when he was 59 and she was 51. Now they live in Punta Gorda, Florida, where they cruise on their 30 foot trawler, play softball and collect shells."

At first, when I read it I thought it might be a joke. A spoof on the American Dream. But it wasn't. Tragically, this was the dream: Come to the end of your life—your one and only precious, God-given life—and let the last great work of your life, before you give an account to your Creator, be this: playing softball and collecting shells.

Picture them before Christ at the great day of judgment: 'Look, Lord. See my shells?' That is a tragedy. And people today are spending billions of dollars to persuade you to embrace that tragic dream. Over against that, I put my protest: Don't buy it. Don't waste your life.[17]

Make It Count

What will you do to share the good news of Jesus?

List **three** people you are praying will accept the gift of salvation:

1. _____

2. _____

3. _____

List **five** people you will invite to be part of this group:

1. _____

2. _____

3. _____

4. _____

5. _____

Commit to sharing the gospel with one person this verse: **but God shows His own love for us in that while we were still sinners, Christ died for us.** (Romans 5:8)

Sharing the gospel is a massively important endeavor because eternity is at stake. Sharing the gospel is also incredibly urgent, since none of us are guaranteed tomorrow. Let these truths frame every decision you make in the days and weeks to come.

CHAPTER SEVEN
THE ULTIMATE
DEFENSE

THROUGHOUT THIS BOOK WE HAVE examined a few arguments in support of the Christian faith. We have also explored the purpose of man and the current human predicament. A life without Jesus Christ only leads to futility and despair. Thus, Jesus alone is the solution to the human predicament: evidence that a personal Creator of the universe exists and that Jesus Christ's offer of eternal life to those who believe in Him is genuine.

But now I want to share with you what I believe to be the most effective and practical defense for the Christian faith. This ultimate defense involves two relationships: your relationship with God and your relationship with others. These two relationships are distinguished by Jesus in His teaching on the duty of man:

Matthew 22:35-40

[35] *And one of them, a lawyer, asked Him a question to test Him.* [36] *"Teacher, which is the great commandment in the Law?"* [37] *And He said to him, "You shall love the Lord your God with all your heart and with all your soul and with all your mind.* [38] *This is the great and first commandment.* [39] *And a second is like it: You shall love your neighbor as yourself.* [40] *On these two commandments depend all the Law and the Prophets."*

The first commandments governs our relationship to God; the second our relationship with our fellow man. Let's examine each of these in turn.

First, our relationship with God. Notice, the importance given in this commandment – loving God is to be our life, not just something we try and do on a Sunday morning. Sometimes we get the idea that the chief end of man is to serve God. However, our primary purpose is to love God. In our relationship with God, He is to have all of us; we are to hold nothing back.

The course of our life is to be totally dedicated to God. Paul, the Apostle, wrote:

Romans 12:1-2

¹ I appeal to you therefore, brothers, by the mercies of God, to present your bodies as a living sacrifice, holy and acceptable to God, which is your spiritual worship. ² Do not be conformed to this world, but be transformed by the renewal of your mind, that by testing you may discern what is the will of God, what is good and acceptable and perfect.

Paul uses the language of the Old Testament ritual offerings that would have been offered up in the Tabernacle or Temple. According to the Law, a Jew would bring his offering of an animal to the priest, who would take it, slay it, and place it on the altar on behalf of the person who brought it.

But the sacrifices required by the Law are no longer of any effect, not even symbolic effect, because when Christ appeared, He fulfilled all the requirements of the Law through His once-for-all, perfect sacrifice. Therefore, sacrifices of dead animals are no longer acceptable to God. The only acceptable offering now is "living," which is the offering up of us to God. We are to surrender to Him all our hopes, plans, and everything that is precious to us. This is what it means to love God.

The other relationship is our relationship with our fellow man. When we choose to love others, we simply show that we have understood God's love for us, and it is being worked out of our lives toward others. What does love involve? To begin with, it means possessing the characteristics of love described in 1 Corinthians 13:

> [4] *Love is patient and kind; love does not envy or boast; it is not arrogant* [5] *or rude. It does not insist on its own way; it is not irritable or resentful;* [6] *it does not rejoice at wrongdoing, but rejoices with the truth.* [7] *Love bears all things, believes all things, hopes all things, endures all things.* [8] *Love never ends....*

True love will have a servant's heart, a willingness to count others as better than self. Jesus is the supreme model, who bowed to wash His disciples' dirty feet.

What will happen from these two relationships is amazing. There will be unity and warmth among Christians. There will be a love that pervades the body of Christ. Furthermore, what will be the result of this unity through love? Jesus Himself gives us the answer:

John 17:21-23

> [21]*that they may all be one, just as You, Father, are in Me, and I in You, that they also may be in Us, so that the world may believe that You have sent Me.* [22] *The glory that You have given Me I have given to them, that they may be one even as We are one,* [23] *I in them and You in Me, that they may become perfectly one, so that the world may know that You sent Me and loved them even as You loved Me.*

According to Jesus, our love is the sign to all people that we truly belong to Jesus. But more than that, our love is living proof to the world that God the Father has sent His Son Jesus Christ and that the Father loves people even as He loves Jesus. When people see this – our love for God manifested in our love for one another – they will in turn be drawn to Christ and will respond to the gospel's offer of salvation.

Love is the ultimate defense of our faith and the ultimate purpose of unvarnished truth.

A LIFE CHANGED

AT THIS POINT I WOULD like to share a small bit of my own personal testimony. I grew up on a farm in rural Southeastern Oklahoma. Together with my mom and my sister, I attended a small country church named Kent Baptist. One Sunday morning after the pastor finished his sermon, my sister went forward to trust Christ as her personal Lord and Savior. I saw that this pleased my mother, so I followed. Within a few weeks she and I were both baptized. However, I really did not want anything to do with Christ, nor did I have desire after this event. Perhaps, needless to say, but later in life I learned that there was nothing genuine about my decision.

At the age of sixteen my mother and father divorced. My father kept the farm and my mother chose to leave. I did not want my mother being on her own, so I went with her. This decision would prove to put a strain on the relationship with my father for many years. After the divorce, my father was working all the time, so I did not see him very much. My mother was working two jobs just to pay the bills. Consequently, I was a young teenage boy with very little parental supervision. Throughout high school and on into my early twenties, I lived a life of sinful rebellion. I was all about self-gratification and nothing else.

My identity was in sports, looks, and what other people thought of me. I always wanted to be known as the tough guy, the guy nobody messed with, so I got into a lot of fights. I was a very angry young man. My whole identity was wrapped up in the things of this world. I was on an emotional rollercoaster that seemed to have no end. After high school I went to work on an offshore drilling rig in the Gulf of Mexico. Money was really good on the rig. I wanted to make as much money as I could. I bought the new truck and had a lot of expensive habits and hobbies. Man, I thought I was something.

As I mentioned before, it was during my time of working offshore that I came face-to-face with death. It's hard to believe that it has been over twenty years since I worked on that rig. You would probably think that after a near death experience like that I would turn my life over to Christ. But I was still obstinate toward the Lord and absorbed in my own fleshly impulses. After my near death experience on the rig, I resigned my position and went to work for the Kiamichi Railroad. Once again, I was making really good money, especially for a young single man. Along with the money came relationships. I jumped from one relationship right into another like most people change shirts. Incredibly enough, now I added relationships to my identity, as I shopped around for significance yet nothing seemed to satisfy. Fulfillment escaped me with every new worldly addition to my life.

It was during this time in my life that I met a beautiful, young woman (Kelly) who is now my wife. While we were dating, I started attending church with her. This went on for about a year and then we were married. Would you believe that after we were married I immediately stopped going to church? I was a diehard genuine hypocrite. The only reason I was going to church was to win her parents over. But as soon as we were married I had no reason to keep going, so I thought.

Kelly was faithful to attend even if I did not go, but I could tell I was pulling her down. Late one Monday night there was a knock on our door. It was a leader from the church Kelly had visited and he wanted to meet me. At the end of our visit, he invited me to church. Reluctantly, the next Sunday I went. Soon one Sunday turned into two, then three and so on. God really began to work on my heart. He began to show me my hypocrisy and my lust for sin. Each time I would hear the gospel it would cut me deeply.

Finally, I could not handle it any longer; I broke under the conviction of the Holy Spirit. I got into my truck and drove to the preacher's house. He invited me in and shared the truth of the gospel with me. The date was April 14, 2000 when I genuinely surrendered my life to Christ for salvation. At that moment, my life changed forever.

ENDNOTES

[1] Doug Powell, *Christian Apologetics* (Nashville: Holman Publications, 2006) pg. 27.

[2] Ibid., 51.

[3] Ibid., 50.

[4] Ibid., 62.

[5] www.preachingtoday.com

[6] J.I. Packer, *Knowing God* (Downers Grove: InterVarsity Press, 1973), 26.

[7] Ibid., 29-31.

[8] Jerry Bridges and Bob Bevington, *The Great Exchange* (Wheaton: Crossway Books, 2007), 21.

[9] Ibid., 37.

[10] www.preachingtoday.com Luis Martinz, *Hero U.S Soldier Gives Life to Save Afghan Girl*, ABC News (3-29-12).

[11] Tony Evans, *Book of Illustrations* (Chicago: Moody Press, 2009), 341.

[12] www.preachtoday.com John Ortberg, *All the Places to Go* (Tyndale House, 2015), page 8; submitted by Kevin Miller, Wheaton, IL.

[13] Dwight D. Eisenhower, *Address at the Second Assembly of the World Council of Churches, Evanston Illinois*, [online] 19 August 1954 [cited 29 October 2015]. Available from the Internet: presidency.ucsb.edu/ws/?pid=9991.

[14] www.preachingtoday.com Adapted from Gabrielle Fonrouge and Selim Algar, "Postal carrier hoarded 40,000 pieces of undelivered mail," New York.

[15] Evans, 77.

[16] Tom Doyle and Greg Webster, *Killing Christians* (Nashville, W Publishing Group, 2015), 16.

[17] John Piper, *Don't Waste Your Life* (Wheaton, IL: Crossway, 2003), 45–6.

For Conferences, Revivals or Speaking Engagements or more information, contact:

Dr. Blake Gideon
1300 E. 33rd St.
Edmond, OK 73013
405-341-0253

www.FBCedmond.org/pastor

www.PastorBlake.com

Additional copies of this book or other books by Dr. Gideon may be purchased at your local bookstore or at most online book sellers, including:

MasterDesign.org

Amazon.com

BN.com

Walmart.com